Easy ~ to ~ Make
CROSS ~ STITCH SAMPLERS
AND MOTTOES

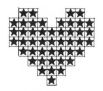

24 Charted Designs by
Barbara Christopher

Dover Publications, Inc.
New York

ACKNOWLEDGMENTS

Much appreciation to DMC for providing the six-strand embroidery floss and Floralia yarn used to work the designs shown on the covers of this book. Thanks to Joan Toggit, Ltd. for supplying the fabric upon which the designs were embroidered; to mail-order these fabrics, write to Hansi's Haus, 246 5th Ave., N.Y., N.Y. 10001.

DEDICATION

To my editor, Linda Macho, for her encouragement and creative help.

Published in Canada by General Publishing Company, Ltd., 30 Lesmill Road, Don Mills, Toronto, Ontario.
Published in the United Kingdom by Constable and Company, Ltd.

Easy-to-Make Cross-Stitch Samplers and Mottoes is a new work, first published by Dover Publications, Inc., in 1984.

International Standard Book Number: 0-486-24664-7

Manufactured in the United States of America
Dover Publications, Inc., 31 East 2nd Street, Mineola, N.Y. 11501

Introduction

Embroidered samplers became popular in the eighteenth century as an educational tool for very young girls and served a dual purpose: they enabled youthful needleworkers to practice the stitches they would be working for the rest of their lives, and at the same time taught them the letters and numbers necessary for marking the family's clothes and household linens (not to actually learn the alphabet, as had once been thought).

In the beginning, embroidered samplers were rather small and simple, displaying little more than a basic alphabet and numbers worked in a variety of useful stitches. They were usually designed by their makers themselves and painstakingly embroidered in counted cross-stitch on very fine linen. As the popularity of samplers grew, decorative elements were added, such as borders, small pictorial representations, biblical quotations and moral sayings. Some Victorian samplers were quite large in order to accommodate the ambitious messages needleworkers of that period wished to include! Nevertheless, samplers long remained a form of education and were often the very first pieces that young girls embroidered in order to perfect and display their skills.

Antique embroidered samplers are acknowledged as genuine examples of folk art, and many are lovingly preserved in homes and museums. Meanwhile, beautiful new samplers are being created by today's needleworkers; no longer merely "diplomas" to be displayed by proud parents, samplers have become popular decorations for the home and cherished gifts. Today's samplers display not only the expert technique of the stitcher, but often reflect the interests and imagination of the maker. A modern sampler can reflect family hobbies, travels and occupations, but perhaps the most popular application is to commemorate an important occasion such as a birth, birthday, baptism, graduation, wedding or anniversary.

The original sampler designs in this collection encompass both traditional and contemporary themes and provide dozens of motifs and borders that are suitable for a wide range of holidays and special occasions, as well as for celebrating friendships and expressing love, gratitude and other happy feelings. You will want to "personalize" some of them by adding names of relatives and friends and appropriate dates. These should be printed by hand on a separate sheet of tissue paper to make sure they fit in the available space. Once you are satisfied with the size and style of your lettering, transfer the words to your fabric using a dressmaker's carbon and a hard lead pencil. Do this *after* the design has been embroidered, so that the lettering can be centered correctly. Embroider the lettering in outline stitch (*diagram 1*).

DIAGRAM 1
Outline Stitch

I would like to make one suggestion about finishing all of the samplers: sign and date your work. In this way, future collectors of beautiful and valuable samplers will have no trouble determining who embroidered the piece they have just purchased at enormous cost! It will also have great meaning for those who receive these samplers as gifts.

Just as the samplers of old served a dual purpose, this book has been designed to appeal to needleworkers who are interested in more than one type of embroidery. Each of the samplers is presented as an easy-to-read color-coded chart, making the designs usable for needlepoint, counted beadwork, latch hooking, crocheting and knitting, as well as counted cross-stitch. My own versions of the completed samplers appear on the covers of this book. I worked the designs in two different techniques—counted cross-stitch and needlepoint—to show the versatility of the charts. You are free to follow my designs exactly (see detailed specifications on the last page of this book) or to experiment with technique and color to create your own adaptations. Next to each chart is a color key indicating the DMC six-strand embroidery floss and/or Floralia Persian yarn that I used. Buy one skein of each color (unless otherwise indicated in parentheses). NOTE: If you are using a technique other than cross-stitch, the skein requirements will need to be adjusted. Many of the color schemes can be simplified without losing any of the beauty of the finished piece; if you decide to simplify, be sure to buy extra skeins of the main colors you have selected.

The technique of counted cross-stitch is simple, and the supplies and equipment required are minimal and inexpensive. You will need:

1. A small blunt tapestry needle, #24 or #26.

2. Evenweave fabric. This can be linen, cotton, wool or a blend that includes miracle fabrics. The three most popular fabrics are:

Cotton Aida. This is made 14 threads per inch, 11 threads per inch, 8 threads per inch, and so forth.

Evenweave Linen. This also comes in a variety of threads per inch. Working on evenweave linen involves a slightly different technique, which is explained on page 5. Thirty-count linen will give a stitch approximately the same size as 14-count Aida.

Hardanger Cloth. This has 22 threads per inch and is available in cotton or linen.

3. Embroidery thread. This can be six-strand mercerized cotton floss (DMC, Coats and Clark, Lily, Anchor, etc.), crewel wool, Danish Flower Thread, silken and metal threads or perle cotton. DMC embroidery floss has been used to color-code the patterns in this book. For 14-count Aida and 30-count linen, divide six-strand cotton floss and work with only two strands. For more texture use more thread. Danish Flower Thread is a thicker thread with a matt finish, one strand equalling two of cotton floss.

4. Embroidery hoop. Use a plastic or wooden 4″, 5″ or 6″ round or oval hoop with a screw type tension adjuster.

5. A pair of sharp embroidery scissors is absolutely essential.

Prepare the fabric by whipping, hemming, or zigzagging on the sewing machine to prevent ravelling at the edges. Next, locate the exact center of the design you have chosen, so that you can then center the design on the piece of fabric. The designs in the book have an arrow at the top and along one side; follow the indicated rows to where they intersect; this is the center stitch. Next, find the center of the fabric by folding it in half both vertically and horizontally. The center stitch of the design should fall where the creases in the fabric meet.

It's usually not very convenient to begin work with the center stitch itself. As a rule, it's better to start at the top of a design working horizontal rows of a single color, left to right. This technique permits you to go from an unoccupied space to an occupied space (from an empty hole to a filled one), which makes ruffling the floss less likely. To find out where the top of the design should be placed, count squares up from the center of the design, and then count off the corresponding number of holes up from the center of the fabric.

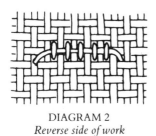

DIAGRAM 2
Reverse side of work

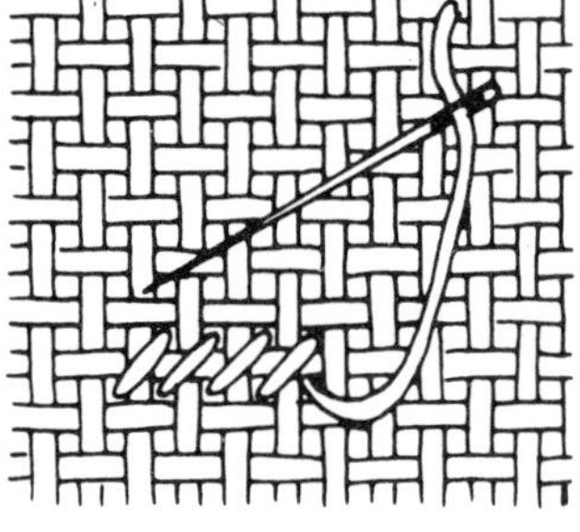

DIAGRAM 3

DIAGRAM 4

DIAGRAM 5

Next, place the section of the fabric to be worked tautly in the hoop; the tighter the better, for tension makes it easier to push the needle through the holes without piercing the fabric. As you work, use the screw adjuster to tighten as necessary. Keep the screw at the top and out of your way. When beginning, fasten the thread with a waste knot by holding a bit of thread on the underside of the work and anchoring it with the first few stitches (*diagram 2*). Do all the stitches in the same color in the same row, working left to right and slanting from bottom left to upper right (*diagram 3*). Then cross back, completing the X's (*diagram 4*). Some cross-stitchers prefer to cross each stitch as they come to it; this is fine, but be sure the slant is always in the correct direction. Of course, isolated stitches must be crossed as you work them. Vertical stitches are crossed as shown in diagram 5. Holes are used more than once; all stitches "hold hands" unless a space is indicated. The work is always held upright, never turned as for some needlepoint stitches.

When carrying a color from one area to another, wiggle your needle under existing stitches on the underside. Do not carry a color across an open expanse of fabric for more than a few stitches as the thread will be visible from the front. Remember, in counted cross-stitch you do not work the background.

To end a color, weave in and out of the underside of the stitches, perhaps making a scallop stitch or two for extra security (*diagram 6*). Whenever possible end in the direction in which you are traveling, jumping up a row, if necessary (*diagram 7*). This prevents holes caused by work being pulled in two directions. Do not make knots; knots make bumps. Cut off the ends of the threads; do not leave any tails because they'll show through when the work is mounted.

The only other stitch used in counted cross-stitch is the backstitch. This is worked from hole to hole and may be vertical, horizontal or slanted (*diagram 8*).

Working on linen requires a slightly different technique. Evenweave linen is remarkably regular, but there are always some thin threads and some that are nubbier or fatter than others. To even these out and to make a stitch that is easy to see, the cross-stitch is worked over two threads each way. The "square" you are covering is thus four threads (*diagram 9*). The first few stitches on linen are sometimes difficult, but

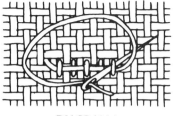

DIAGRAM 6
Reverse side of work

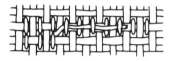

DIAGRAM 7
Reverse side of work

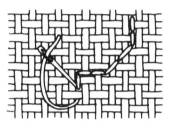

DIAGRAM 8

DIAGRAM 9

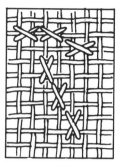

DIAGRAM 10

DIAGRAM 11

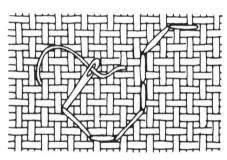

DIAGRAM 12

one quickly begins "to see in twos." After the third stitch, a pattern is established, and should you inadvertently cross over three threads instead of four, the difference in slant will make it immediately apparent that you have erred.

Linen evenweave fabric should be worked with the selvage at the side, not at the top and bottom.

Because you go over more threads, linen affords more variations in stitches. A half cross-stitch can slant in either direction. Diagram 10 shows half cross-stitches worked over one thread in the one direction. A three-quarter cross-stitch is shown in diagram 11. Diagram 12 shows backstitch on linen. A number of the charts in this book were designed specifically for work on linen and call for the use of half cross-stitches and three-quarter cross-stitches. These stitches will have to be worked *between* holes, rather than from hole to hole, when adapted for Aida or Hardanger cloth.

Bear in mind that the finished piece of needlework will not be the same size as the charted design unless you happen to

be working on fabric that has the same number of threads per inch as the chart has squares per inch. To determine how large a finished design will be, divide the number of stitches in the design by the thread-count of the fabric. For example, if a design that is 112 stitches wide by 140 stitches deep is worked on a 14-count cloth, divide 112 stitches by 14 to get 8 and 140 by 14 to get 10; so the worked design will measure 8″ × 10″. The same design worked on 22-count fabric would measure approximately 5″ × 6½″.

After you have completed your embroidery, wash it in cool or lukewarm water with a mild soap. Rinse well. Do not wring. Roll in a towel to remove excess moisture. Immediately iron on a padded surface with the embroidery face down. Be sure the embroidery is completely dry before attempting to mount.

To mount as a picture, center the embroidery over a pure white, rag-content mat board. Turn margins over to the back evenly. Lace the margins with button thread, top to bottom, side to side. The fabric should be tight and even, with a little tension. Never use glue for mounting. Counted cross-stitch on cotton or linen may be framed under glass. Wool needs to breathe and should not be framed under glass unless breathing space is left.

Your local needlework shop or department where you buy your materials will be happy to help you with any problems.

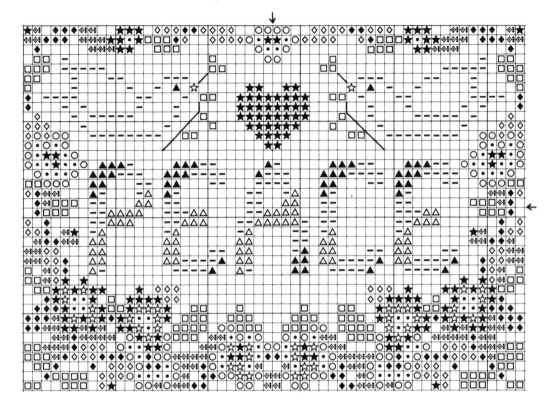

Design 1.

(Embroidery shown on back cover.)

	DMC #
★ bright Christmas red	666
○ medium tangerine	741
• medium yellow	743
△ light blue	813
▲ very dark blue	824
– medium blue	826
□ light parrot green	907
◆ dark emerald green	910
⊗ light emerald green	912
◇ nile green	954
☆ geranium	956

Backstitching: 954

Design 2.

(Embroidery shown on inside back cover.)

		DMC #			DMC #
◆	navy blue	336	☆	bright orange	608
•	dark lemon	444	△	bright chartreuse	704
□	medium Wedgwood	517	−	medium topaz	782
◇	sky blue	519	+	dark coffee brown	801
⊛	dark moss green	580	○	light golden wheat	834
★	dark cranberry	601	▲	medium emerald green	911

Design 3.

(Embroidery shown on inside front cover.)

	DMC #		DMC #
▲ dark hazel nut brown	420	◇ light blue	813
★ bright orange	608	◆ dark blue	825
△ chartreuse	703	• bright canary	973
○ medium tangerine	741	☆ light watermelon	3708

Backstitching: 420

Design 4.

(Embroidery shown on inside back cover.)

		DMC #
✣	light Wedgwood	518
★	medium cranberry	602
□	medium beaver gray	647
○	tangerine	740

		DMC #
•	light tangerine	742
◇	light parrot green	907
♦	very dark avocado green	936

Backstitching: Motto: 936. On butterflies and cats: 647

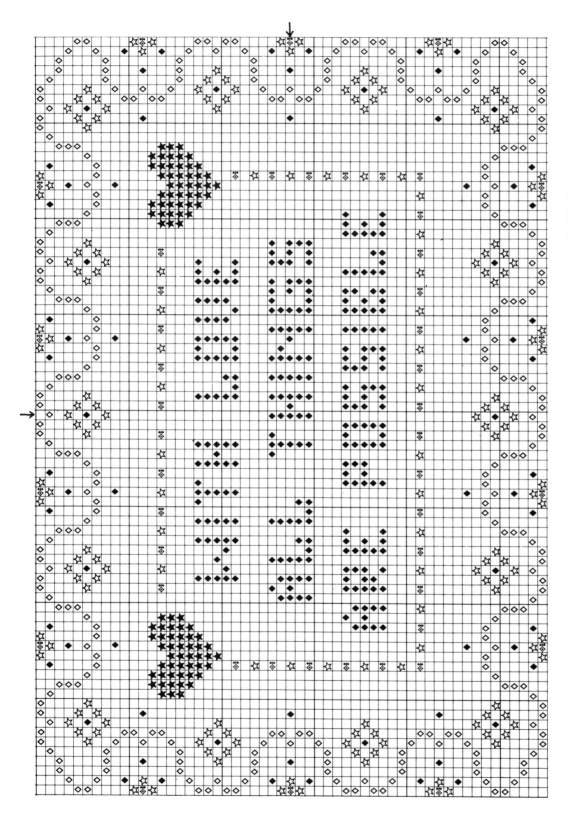

Design 5.

(Embroidery shown on inside front cover.)

DMC #

⊹	medium tangerine	741
★	dark carnation	891
◇	medium nile green	913
◆	medium aquamarine	943
☆	geranium	956

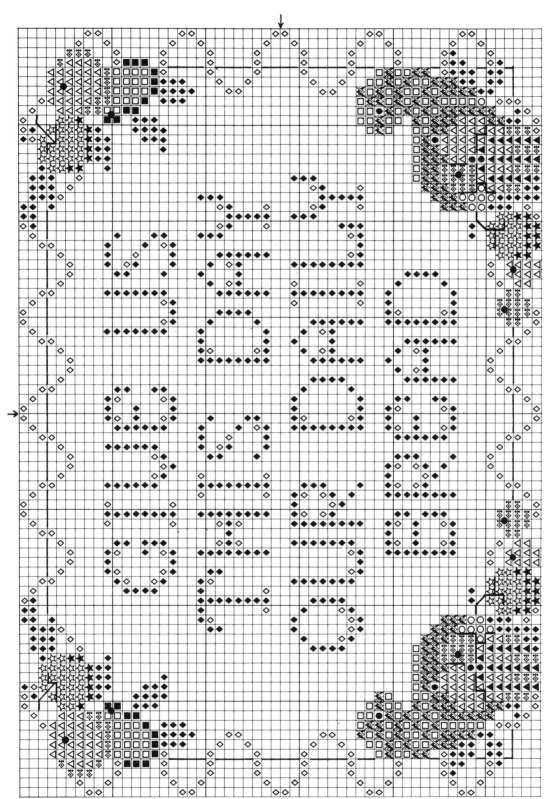

Design 6.

(Embroidery shown on inside front cover.)

	DMC #			DMC #
☆ Christmas red	321	★ medium garnet		815
▲ bright orange	608	◆ dark emerald green		910
△ medium tangerine	741	◇ nile green		954
○ light tangerine	742	✤ light pumpkin		970
■ very dark topaz	780	✕ dark golden brown		975
□ Christmas gold	783			

Backstitching (rectangular border): 741. French knots (indicated by ●): 910

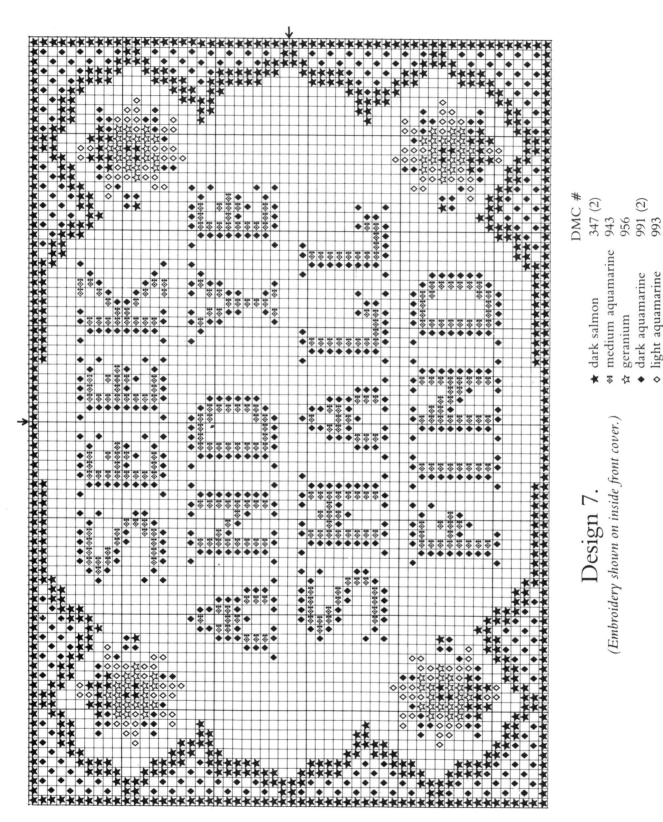

Design 7.

(Embroidery shown on inside front cover.)

		DMC #
★	dark salmon	347 (2)
✤	medium aquamarine	943
☆	geranium	956
◆	dark aquamarine	991 (2)
◇	light aquamarine	993

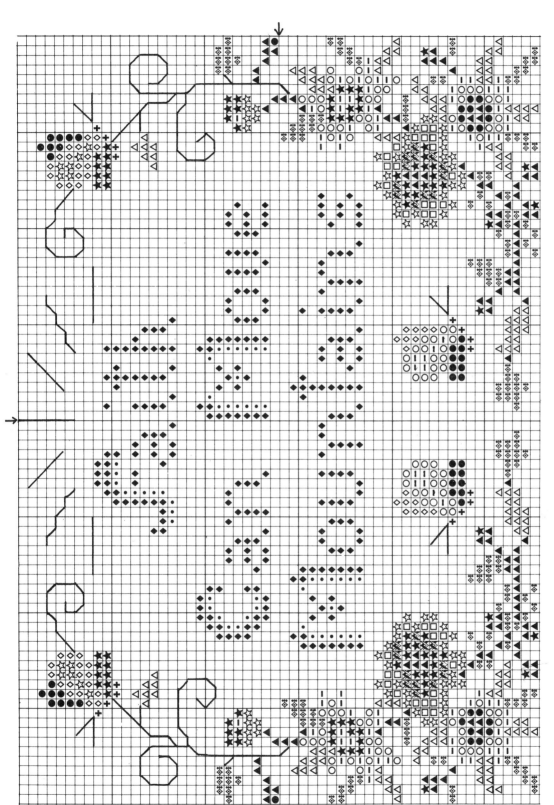

Design 8.

(Embroidery shown on inside back cover.)

	DMC #		DMC #
✳ very dark cranberry	600	△ light parrot green	907
★ medium cranberry	602	✵ nile green	954
☐ cranberry	603	○ light pumpkin	970
☆ very light cranberry	605	✛ medium golden brown	976
● bright orange	608	◆ dark aquamarine	991
– light tangerine	742	◇ baby blue	3325
▲ dark parrot green	905	• gold metallic	

Backstitching: Rays (at top): gold metallic. Flower stems: 905. On blossoms: 976

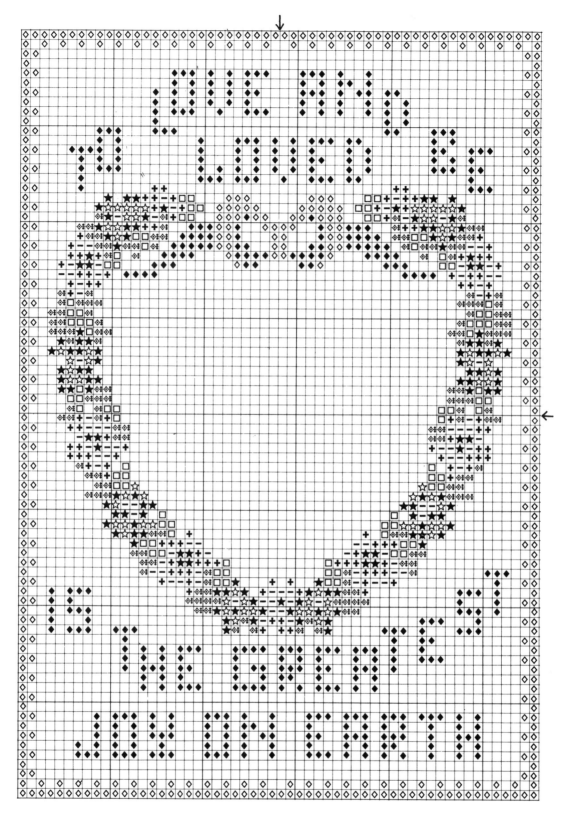

Design 9.

(Embroidery shown on inside front cover.)

		DMC #
+	dark lemon	444
◆	medium Wedgwood	517
☆	cranberry	603
★	bright orange red	606
◇	peacock blue	807
□	light parrot green	907
−	deep canary	972
⬩	light aquamarine	993

Design 10.

(Embroidery shown on inside front cover.)

		DMC #
×	sky blue	519
☆	very light cranberry	605
★	bright Christmas red	666
+	light tangerine	742
–	medium yellow	743
◆	very dark blue	824

		DMC #
◇	medium blue	826
◈	light parrot green	907
▲	dark emerald green	910
○	light pumpkin	970
✕	dark golden brown	975
△	aquamarine	992

Backstitching: Rays (on top) and top and bottom of bird's head: 970.
Bird's beak, and all other: 975

15

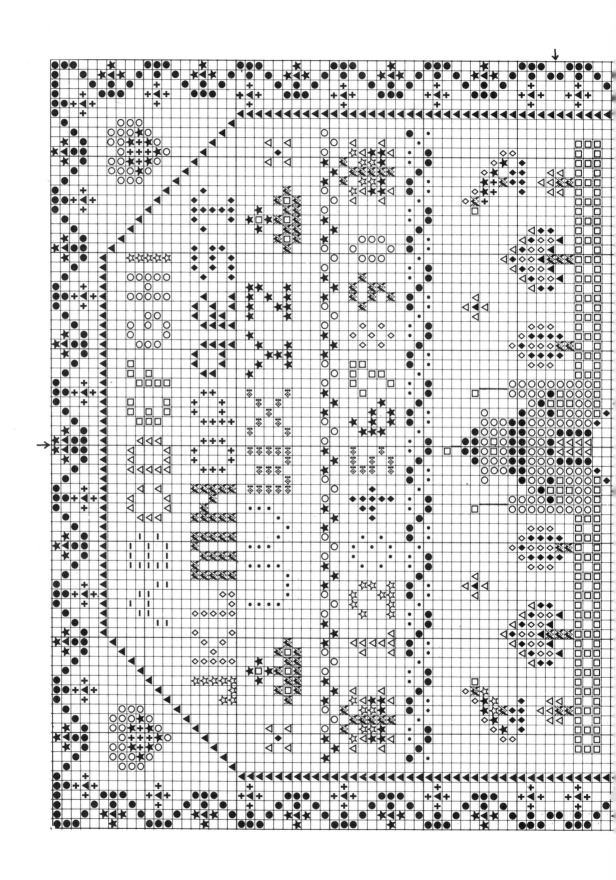

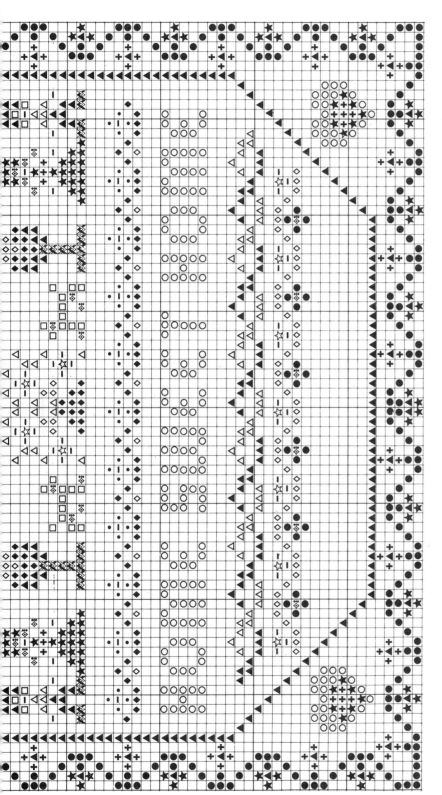

Design 11.

(Embroidery shown on inside front cover.)

DMC #			DMC #	
· sky blue	519	★ dark carnation		891
● very dark violet	550	☆ light carnation		893
◆ dark moss green	580	– very light carnation		894
+ light cranberry	604	◇ light parrot green		907
✳ dark avocado leaf	829	○ medium plum		917
✧ light avocado leaf	831	▲ medium aquamarine		943
□ medium golden wheat	833	△ light aquamarine		993

Backstitching: 917

17

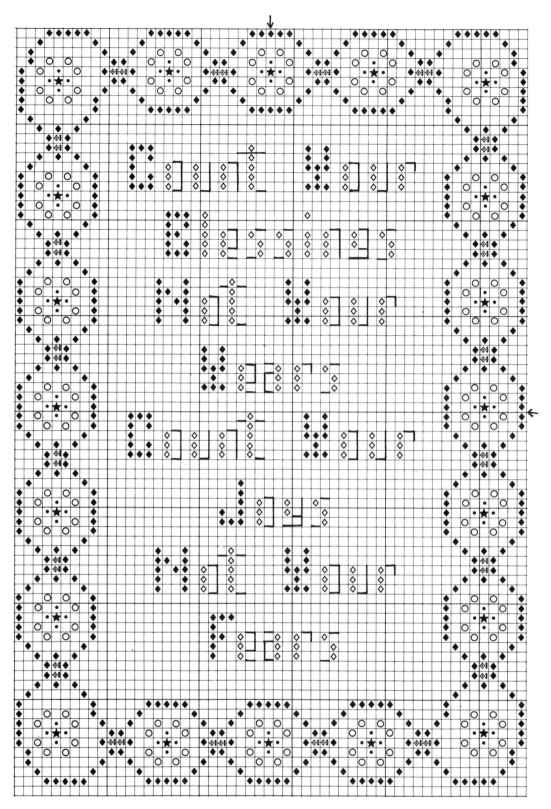

Design 12.

(Embroidery shown on inside back cover.)

		DMC #
◆	medium Wedgwood	517
◇	light Wedgwood	518
★	medium cranberry	602
❈	light parrot green	907
•	deep canary	972
○	melon	3340

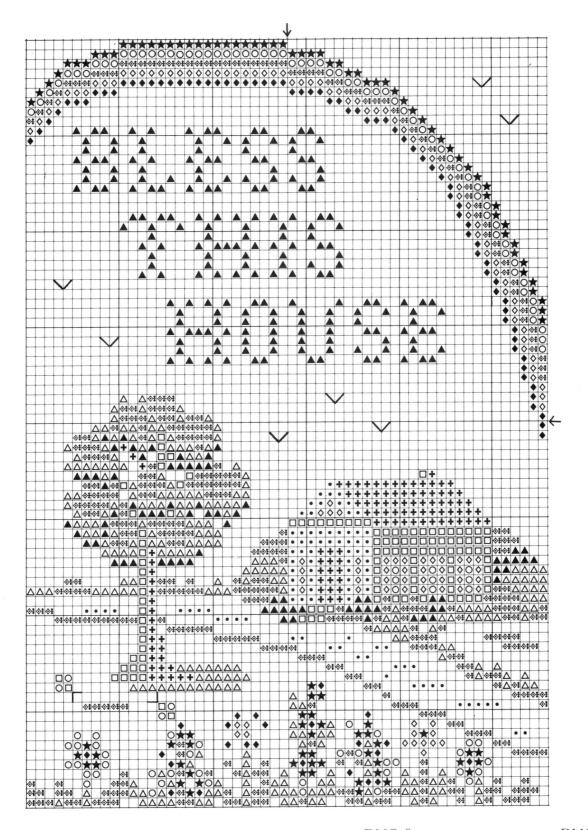

Design 13.

(Embroidery shown on inside back cover.)

	DMC #		DMC #
◆ dark lavender	209	△ kelly green	702
+ very dark mahogany	300	⬙ light parrot green	907
□ very light brown	435	◇ aqua	959
• light tan	437	○ light pumpkin	970
▲ Christmas green	699	★ watermelon	3705

Backstitching: 435

19

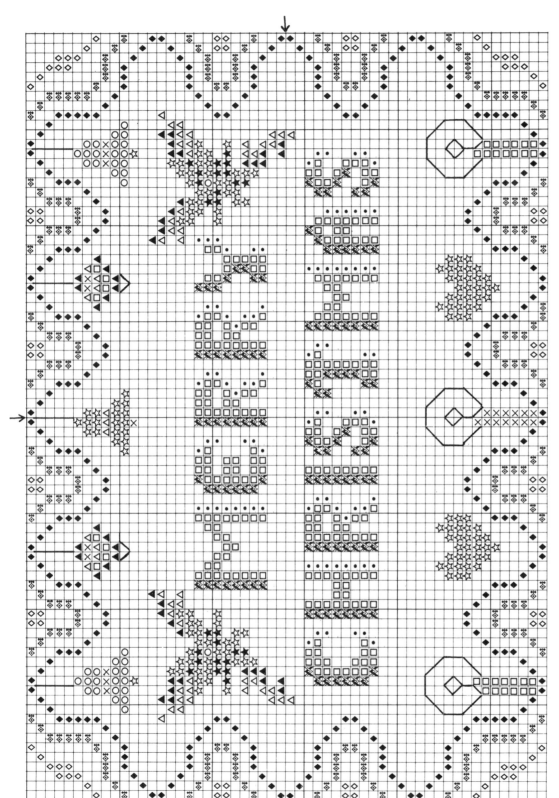

Design 14.

(Embroidery shown on inside back cover.)

	DMC #		DMC #
☆ Christmas red	321	◆ dark blue	825
✕ medium violet	553	◇ ultra very light blue	828
✳ bright orange	608	▲ dark emerald green	910
○ light tangerine	742	△ medium nile green	913
✧ light blue	813	▢ light pumpkin	970
★ medium garnet	815	• gold metallic	

Backstitching: Strings for hanging ornaments: 910. Around candle flames: 321.

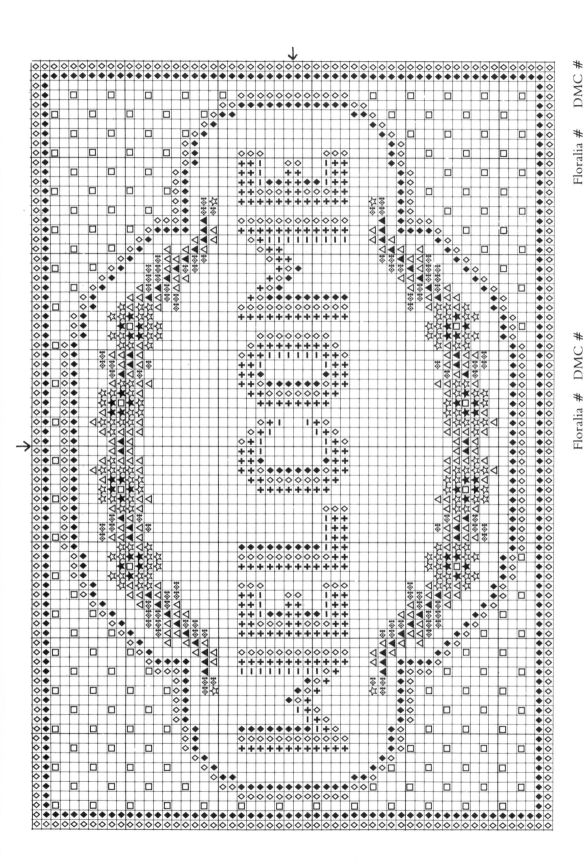

Design 15.

(Embroidery shown on back cover.)

	Floralia #	DMC #
□ medium cocoa brown	7164	407
– light blue	7313	813
◇ medium blue	7314	826
+ dark blue	7317 (2)	825 (2)
✳ medium parrot green	7342	906

	Floralia #	DMC #
▲ dark parrot green	7344	905
◆ very dark blue	7615 (2)	824 (2)
△ light nile green	7754	955
★ cranberry	7804	603
☆ very light cranberry	7818	605

Background coverage only. Center field: ecru (5 skeins).
Outer field: 7120, very light faun brown (5 skeins).

21

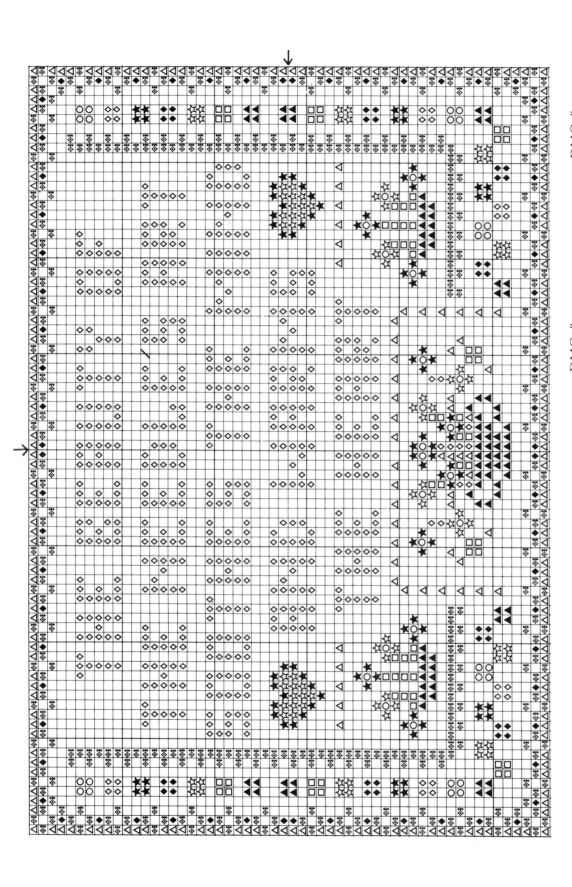

Design 16.

(Embroidery shown on inside back cover.)

	DMC #			DMC #
△ medium cocoa brown	407		◆ dark electric blue	995
▲ chocolate	632		◇ medium electric blue	996
☐ light parrot green	907		★ watermelon	3705
✳ aqua	959		☆ light watermelon	3708
○ deep canary	972			

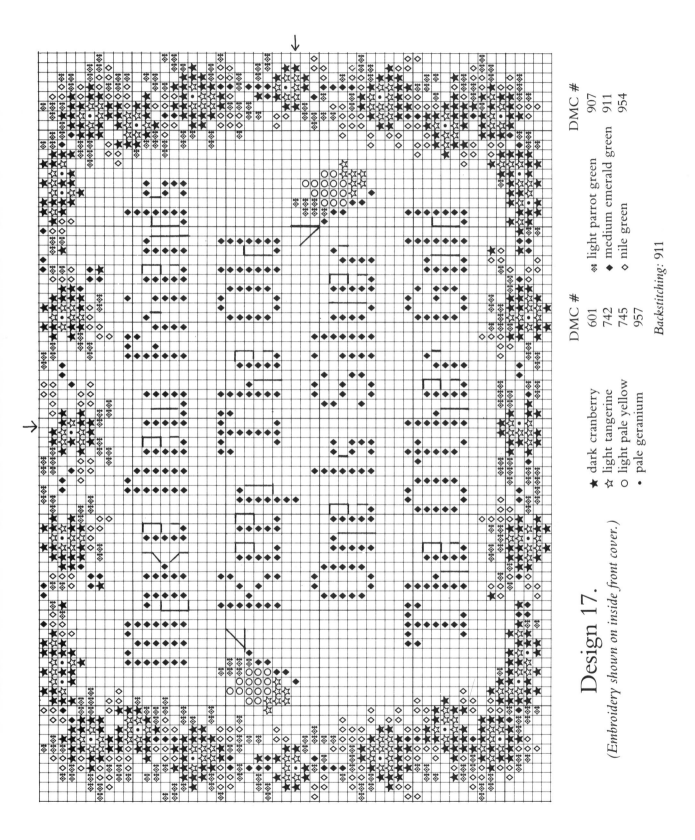

Design 17.

(Embroidery shown on inside front cover.)

DMC #	
★	dark cranberry	601
☆	light tangerine	742
○	light pale yellow	745
•	pale geranium	957

DMC #	
❈	light parrot green	907
◆	medium emerald green	911
◇	nile green	954

Backstitching: 911

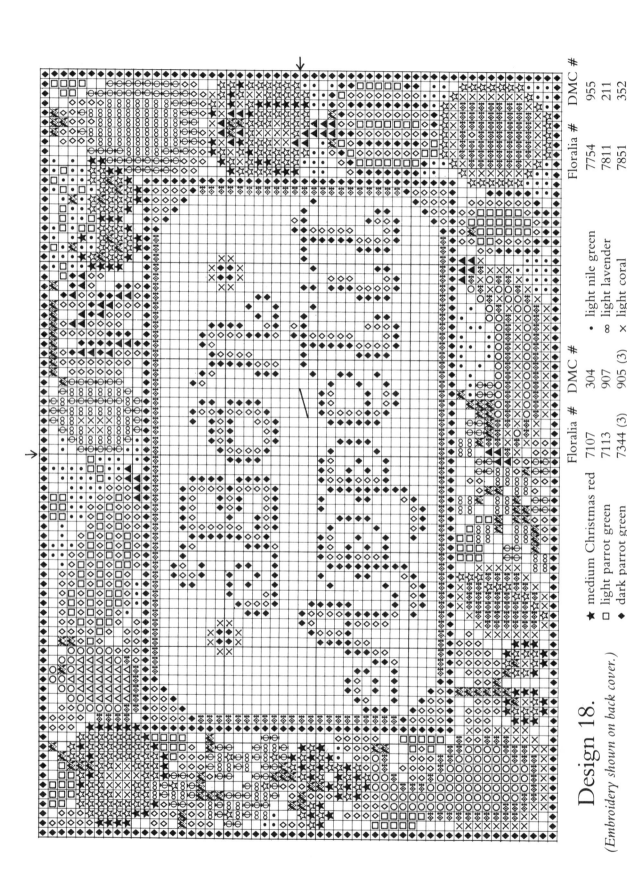

Design 18.

(Embroidery shown on back cover.)

	Floralia #	DMC #
★ medium Christmas red	7107	304
□ light parrot green	7113	907
◆ dark parrot green	7344 (3)	905 (3)
✕ medium brown	7459	433
▲ Christmas gold	7484	783
☆ bright orange red	7606	606
△ light topaz	7726	726

	Floralia #	DMC #
• light nile green	7754	955
∞ light lavender	7811	211
✕ light coral	7851	352
Φ medium violet	7895	553
◇ kelly green	7904 (2)	702 (2)
✳ medium tangerine	7941 (2)	741 (2)
○ bright canary	7972	973

Background coverage only. Center field: 7973, light lemon yellow (4 skeins). Border: 7346, very dark pistachio green (2 skeins) Backstitching (acute accent): Floralia 7344, DMC 905

24

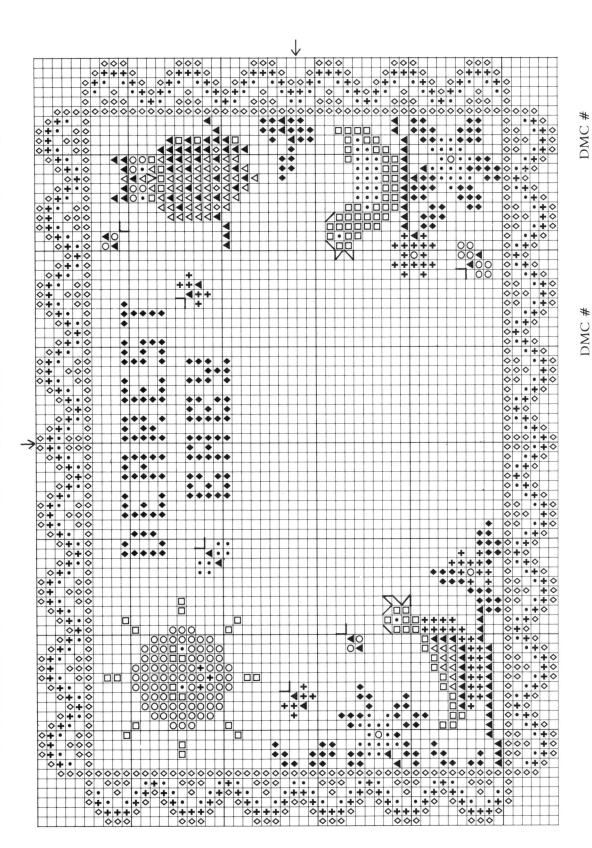

Design 19.

(Embroidery shown on inside back cover.)

	DMC #		DMC #
▲ medium brown	433	△ medium topaz	782
○ dark lemon	444	◆ light parrot green	907
+ cranberry	603	◇ light nile green	954
□ medium tangerine	741	• medium electric blue	996

Backstitching: Flying birds and on butterflies: 433.
Birds' beaks: 603. Tops of birds' heads: 741

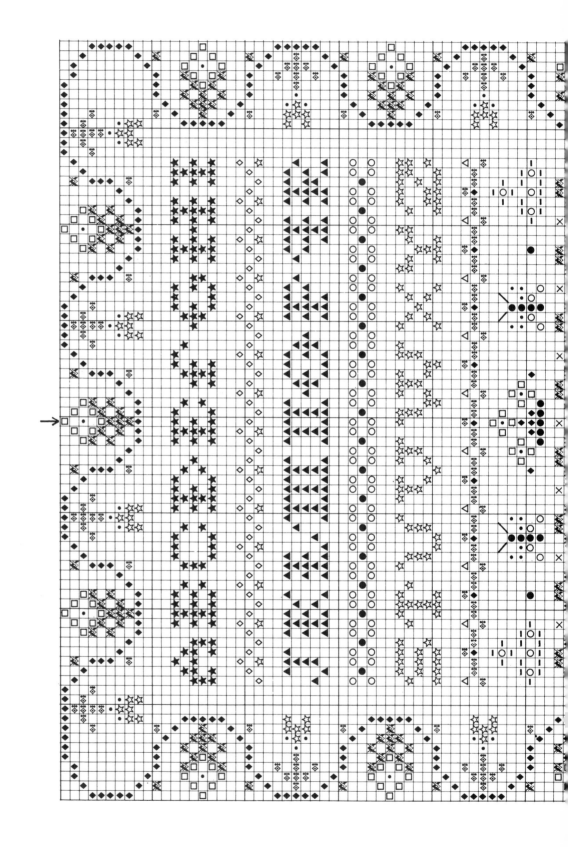

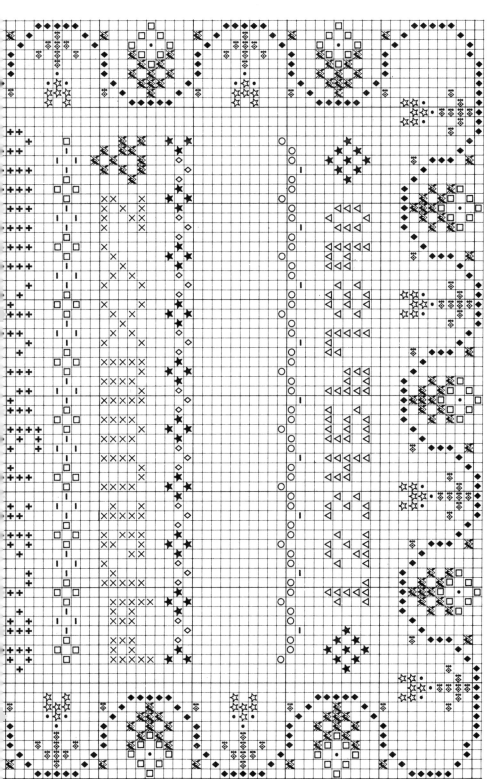

Design 20.

(Embroidery shown on inside back cover.)

	DMC #
× periwinkle blue	340
• dark lemon	444
– medium violet	553
✿ chartreuse	703
+ medium old gold	729
○ light tangerine	742
☆ very light carnation	894
◇ light parrot green	907

	DMC #
● copper	921
▲ aqua	959
△ light aqua	964
◆ dark forest green	987
✖ aquamarine	992
★ spice	3064
□ light melon	3341

Backstitching (on two butterflies): 921

27

Design 21.

(Embroidery shown on inside back cover.)

		DMC #
⋈	medium brown	433
▲	very light brown	435
△	light tan	437
◆	avocado green	469
★	medium cranberry	602
☆	very light cranberry	605
⬥	kelly green	702

		DMC #
○	medium tangerine	741
•	medium yellow	743
◇	light parrot green	907
–	light antique blue	932
+	aqua	959
□	light melon	3341

Backstitching. Alphabet and numerals (at top): 433. Motto: 469.
Outlining doorway in uppermost building: 959. Mouths: 602
French knots (indicated by ●). Both girls' eyes: 959.
Both boys' eyes: 435

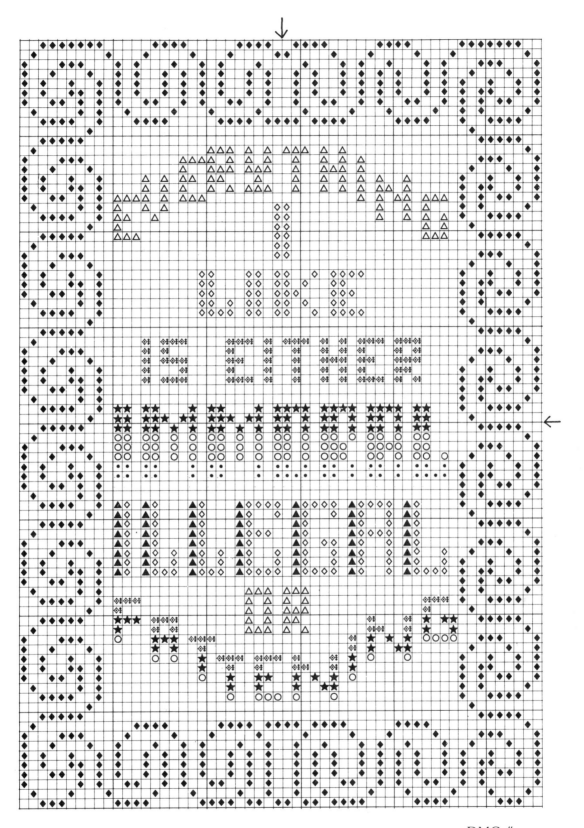

Design 22.

(Embroidery shown on inside front cover.)

		DMC #
★	medium Christmas red	304
◆	medium navy blue	311 (2)
⬧	medium violet	553
△	chartreuse	703
•	light tangerine	742
▲	medium emerald green	911
○	burnt orange	947
◇	medium electric blue	996

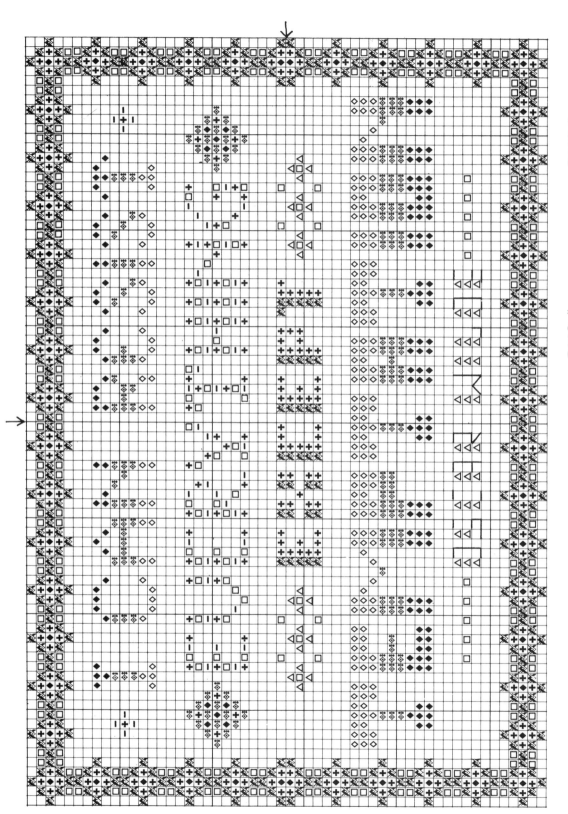

Design 23.

(Embroidery shown on back cover.)

	DMC #		DMC #
△ kelly green	702	✳ medium blue	826
✖ dark coffee brown	801	✛ medium copper	920
◇ light blue	813	▢ burnt orange	947
◆ very dark blue	824	− melon	3340

Backstitching (on signature): 702

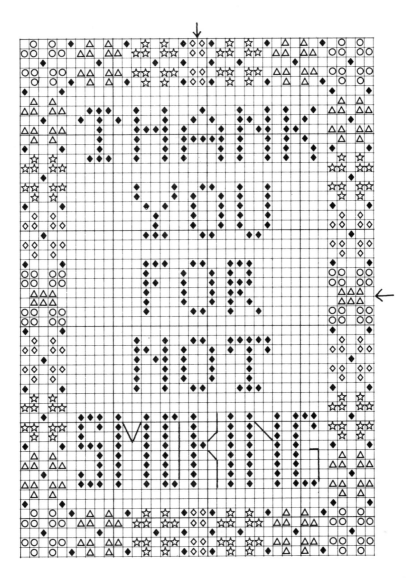

Design 24.

(Embroidery shown on inside front cover.)

		DMC #
○	dark lemon	444
◆	dark navy blue	823
△	light emerald green	912
◇	medium electric blue	996
☆	watermelon	3705

Backstitching: 823

Technical details on the embroideries shown on the covers.

Design 1 (*back cover*). Fabric: "Herta" cotton, 6/1, white. Work over 1 block of threads, using 6 strands of floss. Size: 8½″ × 6″.

Design 2 (*inside back cover*). Fabric: "Belfast" linen, 32/1, white. Work over 4 threads, using 3 strands of floss. Size: 7″ × 10″.

Design 3 (*inside front cover*). Fabric: "Cork" linen, 19/1, white. Work over 2 threads, using 3 strands of floss. Size: 6″ × 8″.

Design 4 (*inside back cover*). Fabric: "Ragusa" poly-acrylic, 14/1, cream. Work over 2 threads, using 3 strands of floss. Size: 7⅜″ × 10″.

Design 5 (*inside front cover*). Fabric: "Almeria" cotton-polyester-linen, natural. Work over 2 threads, using 3 strands of floss. Size: 7¼″ × 5″.

Design 6 (*inside front cover*). Fabric: "Aida" cotton, 14/1, cream. Work over 1 block of threads, using 2 strands of floss. Size: 5¾″ × 4″.

Design 7 (*inside front cover*). Fabric: "Ariosa" rayon-cotton, 20/1, antique rose. Work over 3 threads, using 3 strands of floss. Size: 12″ × 8½″.

Design 8 (*inside back cover*). Fabric: "Cork" linen, 19/1, natural. Work over 2 threads, using 3 strands of floss. Size: 8″ × 5½″.

Design 9 (*inside front cover*). Fabric: "Aida" cotton, 11/1, yellow. Work over 1 block of threads, using 3 strands of floss. Size: 4⅞″ × 7″.

Design 10 (*inside front cover*). Fabric: "Belfast" linen, 32/1, white. Work over 4 threads, using 3 strands of floss. Size: 6⅞″ × 10″.

Design 11 (*inside front cover*). Fabric: "Belfast" linen, 32/1, cream. Work over 4 threads, using 3 strands of floss. Size: 10″ × 13½″.

Design 12 (*inside back cover*). Fabric: "Aida" cotton, 14/1, beige. Work over 1 block of threads, using 2 strands of floss. Size: 3¾″ × 5⅝″.

Design 13 (*inside back cover*). Fabric: "Belfast" linen, 32/1, white. Work over 4 threads, using 3 strands of floss. Size: 6¾″ × 9⅝″.

Design 14 (*inside back cover*). Fabric: "Aida" cotton, 14/1, white. Work over 1 block of threads, using 2 strands of floss. Size: 5½″ × 4″.

Design 15 (*back cover*). Fabric: 10/1 interlock needle-point canvas. Use 3 strands of Persian yarn. Size: 8″ × 5⅝″.

Design 16 (*inside back cover*). Fabric: "Belfast" linen, 32/1, cream. Work over 4 threads, using 3 strands of floss. Size: 9¾″ × 7″.

Design 17 (*inside front cover*). Fabric: "Belfast" linen, 32/1, beige. Work over 4 threads, using 3 strands of floss. Size: 9¾″ × 7⅛″.

Design 18 (*back cover*). Fabric: 10/1 interlock needle-point canvas. Use 3 strands of Persian yarn. Size: 8″ × 5½″.

Design 19 (*inside back cover*). Fabric: "Belfast" linen, 32/1, white. Work over 4 threads, using 3 strands of floss. Size: 9¾″ × 6⅝″.

Design 20 (*inside back cover*). Fabric: "Aida" cotton, 14/1, cream. Work over 1 block of threads, using 2 strands of floss. Size: 5⅝″ × 7⅛″.

Design 21 (*inside back cover*). Fabric: "Aida" cotton, 14/1, white. Work over 1 block of threads, using 2 strands of floss. Size: 4″ × 5½″.

Design 22 (*inside front cover*). Fabric: "Gardasee" poly-acrylic, 14/1, white. Work over 2 threads, using 3 strands of floss. Size: 8″ × 11⅜″.

Design 23 (*back cover*). Fabric: "Ariosa" rayon-cotton, 20/1, yellow. Work over 3 threads, using 3 strands of floss. Size: 12¼″ × 8½″.

Design 24 (*inside front cover*). Fabric: "Aida" cotton, 18/1, medium blue. Work over 2 blocks of threads, using 3 strands of floss. Size: 4⅛″ × 6″.